celebrate

CONSTITUTION DAY WITHDRAWN

BY Barbara deRubertis

The Kane Press
New York

D0927540

For activities and resources for this book and
others in the HOLIDAYS & HEROES series, visit:
www.kanepress.com/holidays-and-heroes

Acknowledgments: With special thanks to the staff at the National
Constitution Center in Philadelphia, PA.

Text copyright © 2015 by Barbara deRubertis
Photographs/images copyrights: Cover: © Michael Ventura/Alamy; page 1: © bonnie jacobs/iStock; page
3 top: © wavebreakmedia/Shutterstock.com; page 3 bottom: © bonnie jacobs/iStock; page 4 top: Library
of Congress, Prints & Photographs Division, LC-USZ62-7819; page 4 bottom: © Pictorial Press Ltd/
Alamy; page 5: © North Wind Picture Archives -- All rights reserved; page 6: Library of Congress, Prints
& Photographs Division, LC-DIG-ds-00123; page 7: Library of Congress, Prints & Photographs Division,
LC-DIG-ds-00688; page 8: © North Wind Picture Archives -- All rights reserved; page 9: © Everett
Historical/Shutterstock.com; pages 10–11: © Picture History/Newscom; pages 12–13 (left to right): ©
trekandshoot/Shutterstock.com, © Brandon Bourdages/Shutterstock.com, © Orhan Cam/Shutterstock.com;
page 14: © Everett Collection Historical/Alamy; page 15: Photo by Jim Steinhart. © 2015 Jim Steinhart of
TravelPhotoBase.com, all rights reserved. (Ref: WIMC325); pages 16–17: © ClassicStock/Alamy; page 18
top: © yurchello108/Shutterstock.com; page 18 bottom: © Joseph Sohm/Visions of America/Corbis; page 19:
© AleksandarNakic/iStock; page 20: © North Wind Picture Archives -- All rights reserved; page 21: Library
of Congress, Prints & Photographs Division, LC-DIG-ds-04435; page 22 & 23: © North Wind Picture
Archives -- All rights reserved; page 24: © leezsnow/iStock; page 25 top left: © Joseph Sohm/Shutterstock.
com; page 25 top right: © Dennis Steen/Shutterstock.com; page 25 bottom left: © Monkey Business Images/
Shutterstock.com; page 25 bottom right: © ninjaMonkeyStudio/iStock; page 26 top: © Everett Historical/
Shutterstock.com; page 26 bottom: © traveler1116/iStock; page 27: © Hill Street Studios Blend Images/
Newscom; page 28 left: © ZUMA Press, Inc./Alamy; page 28 right: © Brian Cahn/ZUMAPress/Newscom;
page 29: © John Angellilo/UPI/Newscom; page 30: © Aurelia Ventura/La Opinion/Newscom; page 31:
© Michael Ventura/Alamy; page 32 top: © Shannon Stapleton/Reuters/Newscom; page 32 bottom: ©
Rawpixel/Shutterstock.com
All due diligence has been conducted in identifying copyright holders and obtaining permissions.

Library of Congress Cataloging-in-Publication Data

deRubertis, Barbara.
  Let's celebrate Constitution Day / by Barbara deRubertis.
    pages cm. — (Holidays & heroes)
  Audience: Ages 6-10.
  ISBN 978-1-57565-814-8 (library reinforced binding : alk. paper) — ISBN 978-1-57565-749-3 (pbk. :
alk. paper)
  1. Constitution Day and Citizenship Day (U.S.)—Juvenile literature. 2. United States. Constitution—
Anniversaries, etc.—Juvenile literature. 3. United States--Politics and government—1783-1789—
Juvenile literature. 4. Constitutional history—United States—Juvenile literature. I. Title.
  E303.D46 2015
  394.263—dc23
                              2015012885

eISBN: 978-1-57565-750-9

1 2 3 4 5 6 7 8 9 10

First published in the United States of America in 2015 by Kane Press, Inc. Printed in the USA.
Book Design: Edward Miller. Photograph/Image Research: Poyee Oster.

Visit us online at www.kanepress.com.

Like us on Facebook
facebook.com/kanepress

Follow us on Twitter
@KanePress

Every year on September 17 we celebrate the signing of the Constitution of the United States of America. The Constitution is our nation's most important document. It lays out the basic rules for how our government works. And it protects our rights and freedoms as citizens.

No wonder we Americans are so proud of our Constitution!

But writing the Constitution was not easy. . . .

The writers of the Constitution worked hard—and argued about many things. But on one point the writers all agreed: they did *not* want an all-powerful king. They had had enough of that when they were British colonists. They all felt strongly that power should rest in the hands of the *people*.

King George III was the ruler of Great Britain during the American Revolution.

When and why did Americans decide they needed a constitution? What led up to the writing of this important document?

American colonists in Boston in the 1700s

4

To answer these questions, we need to go back to the time before America declared its independence.

The 13 American colonies belonged to Great Britain. But by 1775, people in the colonies were becoming more and more unhappy with rule by the British king. The colonists had no voice in their government—none at all. The Revolutionary War broke out between the American colonists and the British.

The colonists signed a Declaration of Independence on July 4, 1776. The next year, these newly "united states" drew up the Articles of Confederation, or rules, for their new government.

During this time, General George Washington served as Commander-in-Chief of the United States Army. The Revolutionary War lasted eight long years, from 1775 until 1783. But at last, the United States won its freedom.

Left: George Washington

Above: A battle at sea during the Revolutionary War

By 1787, the new government of the United States of America was having a lot of problems operating under the Articles of Confederation. No one was "in charge" of running the government. Decisions were not being made. Money was needed to run the country—but the government had no way to collect taxes.

So a convention was called to solve these problems.

The Constitutional Convention took place at the State House in Philadelphia, PA, which was later renamed Independence Hall.

James Madison

All the states except Rhode Island sent delegates to the Constitutional Convention in Philadelphia. Some delegates wanted to try to fix the Articles of Confederation. Others wanted to write an entirely new constitution. But *everyone* wanted George Washington to preside over the convention.

James Madison took notes during every meeting . . . for 16 weeks! His own ideas were so valuable, he is often called the "Father of the Constitution."

There were many disagreements about how the government should work. The biggest disagreement was about how to balance power. Who should have most of the power—the states or the federal government?

Another disagreement was about how many representatives each state should have in Congress. States with larger populations preferred the Virginia Plan, which would give more representatives to states with bigger populations.

States with smaller populations preferred the New Jersey Plan, which would give all states the same number of representatives.

Roger Sherman, a delegate from Connecticut, suggested a compromise. Congress should be divided into two parts. In the Senate, states would have equal representation. But in the House of Representatives, representation would be based on population. This was called the Connecticut Compromise.

A group of delegates presents ideas before George Washington at the Constitutional Convention.

There were many other important debates. For example, how should power be divided among the three branches of government? It was decided to create a system of "checks and balances," like a three-legged stool.

★ The legislative branch (Congress) would make the laws.

★ The judicial branch (the Courts) would interpret the laws.

★ The executive branch (the President) would enforce the laws.

Congress meets in the U.S. Capitol building.

The Supreme Court Building

In this way, no single branch would have too much power. Each branch would be kept "in check" by the other two branches. And all three legs of the stool would be balanced!

The president lives and works in the White House.

The most important part missing from the new Constitution was the protection of people's specific, individual rights— a "Bill of Rights." This was a great concern for some delegates, but it would have to be dealt with later.

After four months of difficult work, the new Constitution was finished. It was ready for signing by the convention delegates on September 17, 1787.

Alexander Hamilton, a delegate from New York, was a persuasive supporter of the new Constitution, even though he thought it was far from perfect. He encouraged all the delegates to sign it.

Alexander Hamilton encouraged delegates to sign the new Constitution.

Delegates sign the Constitution.

But three delegates refused to sign. Two of them thought a Bill of Rights should have been included. One thought the executive branch should be a three-man council instead of a one-man president!

The final result was that the Constitution was signed by 39 of the original 55 delegates (some delegates had already gone home). George Washington signed first. All those who signed either the Declaration of Independence or the Constitution are now called the "Founding Fathers" of our country.

Probably none of the delegates was completely happy with this new Constitution. It was the result of many compromises. But it spelled out ways it could be "amended," or changed, in the future. So it would prove to be a surprisingly useful and long-lasting document!

The signing of the Constitution

From time to time during the convention, Benjamin Franklin had thought about the "half-sun" carved into the top of George Washington's chair. Was it a rising sun or a setting sun? Would this new nation succeed—or would it soon come to an end? With the

Benjamin Franklin

signing of the Constitution, Franklin decided the half-sun was definitely a rising sun!

George Washington's "rising sun" armchair

The time had come for each of the states to "ratify," or vote to approve, the Constitution. This document had been written in secrecy, but now it was made public. State conventions were held where people could vote "yes" or "no."

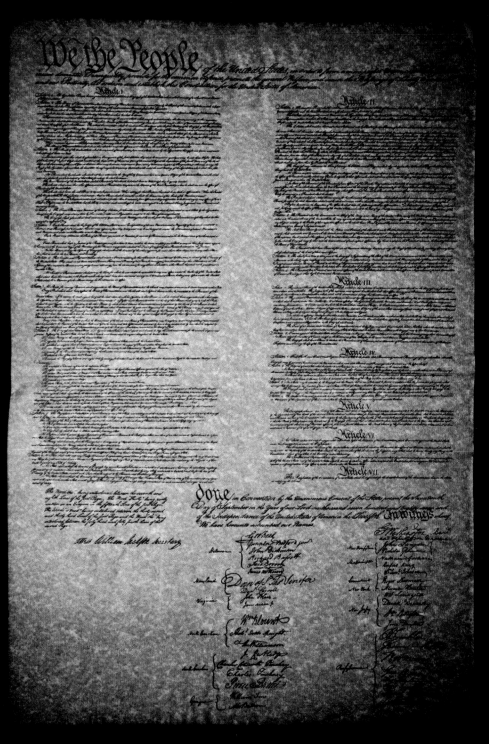

The full text of the Constitution and all 39 signatures are displayed here on a single
page, rather than the original four pages.

There was serious criticism of the Constitution. Some people said the delegates had gone too far. They should only have improved on the old Articles of Confederation, not written an entirely new Constitution. Some complained that there was no Bill of Rights. Another group complained that the new Constitution gave too much power to the federal government and took away power from the states.

Alexander
Hamilton

Alexander Hamilton again put his persuasive powers to use. He supported having a strong federal government, so he was called a "federalist." He wrote most of the 85 important essays now known as "The Federalist Papers." James Madison and John Jay wrote the others. These essays helped win support for the Constitution in several key states.

The Constitution went into effect as soon as 9 of the 13 states (a two-thirds majority) had ratified it—on June 21, 1788. Huge celebrations were held two weeks later, on the 4th of July, with parades and speeches and bonfires.

New York celebrates the adoption of the Constitution with a parade honoring Alexander Hamilton.

Washington is sworn in as president in New York City in 1789.

On April 30, 1789, George Washington took the oath of office as the first president under the new Constitution. In the election, *all* the electors had voted for Washington!

Bill of Rights

Congress OF THE United States,

begun and held at the City of New York, on Wednesday, the fourth of March, one thousand seven hundred and eighty nine.

The Conventions of a number of the States having, at the time of their adopting the Constitution, expressed a desire, in order to prevent misconstruction or abuse of its powers, that further declaratory and restrictive clauses should be added: And as extending the ground of public confidence in the Government, will best insure the beneficent ends of its institution:

Resolved, by the SENATE and HOUSE of REPRESENTATIVES of the UNITED STATES of AMERICA in Congress assembled, two thirds of both Houses concurring, That the following Articles be proposed to the Legislatures of the several States, as Amendments to the Constitution of the United States; all, or any of which articles, when ratified by three fourths of the said Legislatures, to be valid to all intents and purposes, as part of the said Constitution, viz.

Articles in addition to, and Amendment of the Constitution of the United States of America, proposed by Congress, and ratified by the Legislatures of the several States, pursuant to the fifth Article of the Original Constitution.

Article the first ...... After the first enumeration required by the first Article of the Constitution, there shall be one Representative for every thirty thousand, until the number shall amount to one hundred, after which, the proportion shall be so regulated by Congress, that there shall be not less than one hundred Representatives, nor less than one Representative for every forty thousand persons, until the number of Representatives shall amount to two hundred, after which, the proportion shall be so regulated by Congress, that there shall not be less than two hundred Representatives, nor more than one Representative for every fifty thousand persons. [Not Ratified]

Article the second .... No law, varying the compensation for the services of the Senators and Representatives, shall take effect, until an election of Representatives shall have intervened. [Not Ratified]

Article the third .... Congress shall make no law respecting an establishment of religion, or prohibiting the free exercise thereof; or abridging the freedom of speech, or of the press; or the right of the people peaceably to assemble, and to petition the Government for a redress of grievances.

Article the fourth ..... A well regulated Militia, being necessary to the security of a free State, the right of the people to keep and bear Arms, shall not be infringed.

Article the fifth .... No Soldier shall, in time of peace, be quartered in any house, without the consent of the owner, nor in time of war, but in a manner to be prescribed by law.

Article the sixth .... The right of the people to be secure in their persons, houses, papers, and effects, against unreasonable searches and seizures, shall not be violated, and no Warrants shall issue but upon probable cause, supported by oath or affirmation, and particularly describing the place to be searched, and the persons or things to be seized.

Article the seventh ... No person shall be held to answer for a capital, or otherwise infamous crime, unless on a presentment or indictment of a grand jury, except in cases arising in the land or Naval forces, or in the Militia, when in actual service in time of War or public danger; nor shall any person be subject for the same offence to be twice put in jeopardy of life or limb; nor shall be compelled in any criminal case, to be a witness against himself, nor be deprived of life, liberty, or property, without due process of law; nor shall private property be taken for public use without just compensation.

Article the eighth ..... In all criminal prosecutions, the accused shall enjoy the right to a speedy and public trial by an impartial jury of the State and district wherein the crime shall have been committed, which district shall have been previously ascertained by law, and to be informed of the nature and cause of the accusation; to be confronted with the witnesses against him; to have compulsory process for obtaining witnesses in his favor, and to have the assistance of counsel for his defence.

Article the ninth .... In suits at common law, where the value in controversy shall exceed twenty dollars, the right of trial by jury shall be preserved, and no fact, tried by a jury, shall be otherwise re-examined in any Court of the United States, than according to the rules of the common law.

Article the tenth ...... Excessive bail shall not be required, nor excessive fines imposed, nor cruel and unusual punishments inflicted.

Article the eleventh .. The enumeration in the Constitution, of certain rights, shall not be construed to deny or disparage others retained by the people.

Article the twelfth .... The powers not delegated to the United States by the Constitution, nor prohibited by it to the States, are reserved to the States respectively, or to the people.

ATTEST,

Frederick Augustus Muhlenberg Speaker of the House of Representatives.

John Adams, Vice-President of the United States, and President of the Senate.

John Beckley, Clerk of the House of Representatives.

Sam. A. Otis Secretary of the Senate.

Also in 1789, the first meeting of Congress was held. James Madison introduced 12 Amendments, or additions, he hoped to make to the Constitution. The 10 Amendments that were finally adopted are known as the "Bill of Rights."

Some of the individual rights protected in the Bill of Rights are

★ freedom of religion,

★ freedom of speech,

★ freedom of assembly, and

★ freedom of the press.

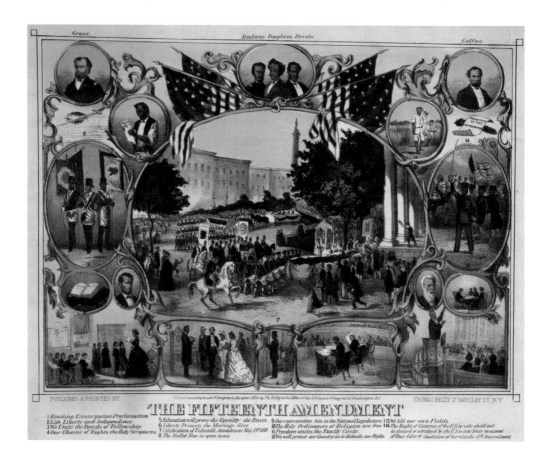

THE FIFTEENTH AMENDMENT

Another 17 Amendments have been added over the years, allowing the Constitution to continue to grow and change with the times.

Amendments 11 through 27 guarantee important freedoms such as

★ abolishing slavery,
★ giving all races the right to vote, and
★ giving women the right to vote.

For over 200 years, the Constitution has served the people of the United States well, even as we have grown from 13 states to 50. Many people in the world do not enjoy the same rights and freedoms that our Constitution gives us. It is important to understand and appreciate these freedoms—and to appreciate all the men and women who have protected these freedoms over the years.

In 2004, a federal law was passed naming September 17 **Constitution Day and Citizenship Day**. The "Constitution Day" part of the holiday is celebrated in schools by teaching students about the Constitution. The "Citizenship Day" part of the holiday honors all those who have become—or are about to become—American citizens.

A boy dresses up for Constitution Day at school.

Children recite the Pledge of Allegiance at a Constitution Day event.

How does someone become an American citizen? There are three ways.

★ Everyone born in the U.S. is a citizen.

★ Those born outside the U.S. are citizens if at least one parent is a citizen.

★ Others may become citizens by following the steps to "naturalized" citizenship. The steps include having a background check and passing tests in English and in U.S. history and government.

A young girl at an oath-taking ceremony. Children become citizens when a parent becomes a naturalized citizen.

Naturalization ceremonies for new citizens are held throughout the year, but a great many are held on or near September 17. During these ceremonies, people who have qualified for citizenship take an Oath of Allegiance to the United States and its Constitution. From that moment on, they enjoy all the rights and responsibilities of being citizens!

People become U.S. citizens at a naturalization ceremony.

Visitors at the National Archives look at the original Constitution.

There's another fine way to celebrate Constitution Day and Citizenship Day if you are near Washington, D.C. You can see the original Constitution, Bill of Rights, and Declaration of Independence at the National Archives!

And if you are near Philadelphia, you can visit the National Constitution Center. Established by Congress, this center brings the story of our Constitution to life. You can also visit their website to learn more about the Constitution.

The greatest strength of our United States Constitution is that it puts power in the hands of the people. Also, it balances power between the states and the federal government. It separates the powers of the legislative, judicial, and executive branches. It sets up a system of checks and balances so that no single branch has too much power. And it protects the individual freedoms of our citizens.

This is *all* worth celebrating every year on September 17!

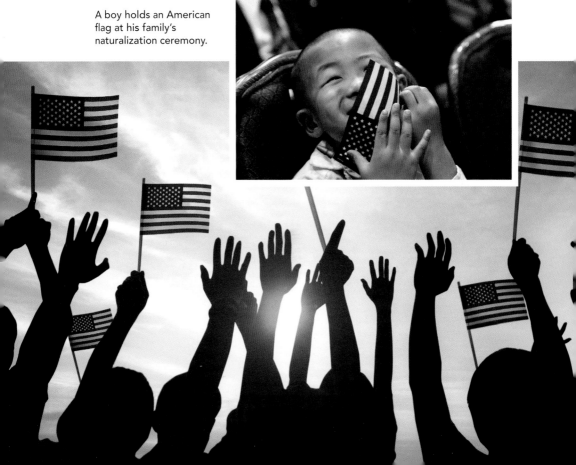

A boy holds an American flag at his family's naturalization ceremony.